MW00980720

For Ter
I love you so!
much –
Amelia Diaz
Ettinger

SPEAKING AT A TIME
HABLANDO A LA VEZ

PRAISE FOR *SPEAKING AT A TIME*

"In *Speaking At A Time*, Amelia Díaz Ettinger first celebrates growing up in 1960s Puerto Rico. She names what she loves–the island's tropical riches, the lives of those who loved her, the daily facts of working people. In forthright bi-lingual vernacular, the poems catalog her urban childhood and adolescence in Caguas—a physician's daughter thriving in a multi-cultural milieu. Evenings, she listened to her father and uncles reciting Hispanic poetry. On television, she heard Pales Matos and Nicolas Guillen. At school she learned to write her own poems. When she immigrated to the United States in 1974, and began her quest for an education, love, career, marriage, family, everything changed. In the 1990s, while raising her children far from any community of Puerto Rican writers or poets such as those Nuyoricans who publish their experiences in the United States, she realized that her immigrant quest had created great cultural and linguistic distance between herself and her children. So, the later poems develop conflicts between immigration and integration, between Anglo and Hispanic cultures, between alienation and community. To resolve those conflicts, the poet synthesizes cultures and languages, best symbolized by the book's bi-lingual presentation, while she continues to document and question what it means to be a Puerto Rican exile in Oregon. This is strong and honest work—filled with love and grief and eloquence. With these solo pages, she joins her distant contemporaries—Victor Hernandez Cruz, Judith Ortiz Cofer, Tato Laviera."

—GEORGE VENN, Eastern Oregon University,
General Editor, *Oregon Literature Series*

"Amelia Díaz Ettinger's book of poems, *Speaking at a Time*, is a gathering of poems about her father, her daughter, the town of Caguas, and the race track, among other things. These recollections pulse with energy, and they echo the poetry of Lorca and Neruda. This is a strong, first book."

—PETER SEARS, Oregon Poet Laureate

REDBAT BOOKS ✦ PACIFIC NORTHWEST WRITERS SERIES

AMELIA DÍAZ ETTINGER

SPEAKING AT A TIME

POEMS

HABLANDO A LA VEZ

redbat
books

redbat books
2015

Copyright © 2015 by Amelia Díaz Ettinger

All rights reserved. This book or any portion thereof may not be reproduced or used in any manner whatsoever without the express written permission of the publisher except for the use of brief quotations in a book review.

Printed in the United States of America

First Trade Paperback Edition: August 1, 2015

ISBN 978-0-9895924-3-7
Library of Congress Control Number: 2015943808

Published by
redbat books
2901 Gekeler Lane
La Grande, OR 97850
www.redbatbooks.com

Text set in Garamond Premier Pro.

Book design by Kristin Summers, redbat design | www.redbatdesign.com

TABLE OF CONTENTS

PART III

PART 1 | PARTE 1

ODE TO THE MANGO

Don Pablo Neruda gave me the watermelon
but my father gave me the mango.
How unlike the green whale of summer!
An impossible shape—
not round or elongated
asymmetrical
tight and smooth
adolescent
coy
sensual
timid
so alluring.
In the trees
it hangs
in bunches.
Your eye sees the one
beckoning—*Come and get me.*
She wants to feel your face
neck
nipples
to be eaten at the beach
in a bathing suit
with the wind undulating.
The slain
make you wait
and admire her insides
a solar plexus!
How she flows
runs
embraces.
Wild, she is
a boxer
compact
leaving

ODA AL MANGÓ

Don Pablo Neruda me dio la sandía
pero Papi me dio el mangó.
¡Tan diferente a la gran ballena de verano!
Una forma imposible de verdad—
ni redonda ni alargada
asimétrica
durita y tierna
adolescente
coqueta
seductora
tímida
tan atractiva.
En árboles cuelga
en racimos.
Tú ojo la ve
señalándote—*Ven y cójeme.*
Ella quiere sentir tu cara
cuello
pezones
para comérsela en la playa
en un traje de baño
con el viento ululando.
La escogida
te hace esperar
que admires sus entrañas
¡un plexo solar!
Como se entrega
corre
abraza.
Silvestre, es
una boxeadora
compacta
dejando

tentacles in tight spaces.
But a graft,
oh graft!
Botanical marvel
she is tall and plump
quinceañera
ready to celebrate her birthday
so the whites wonder at the flesh
so unlike the others—
it slips
it slobbers
it satisfies.

tentáculos en lugares apretados.
Pero un injerto,
¡ay injerto!
Maravilla botánica
es alta y gordita
una quinceañera
lista para celebrar su cumpleaños
y los blancos se maravillan con su piel
tan diferente a las otras—
resbala
babea
satisface.

ODE TO THE PLANTAIN

Oh, fool conquistador
why did the potato with its dirty baby skin

with a form so banal and undignified
become the world's most wanted staple

when under your aquiline nose grew
the green, phallic, magnificent

plantain!
Skin of steel that demands a machete

didn't you see its lovely shape—
hard, manly, and aroused?

Multitude of colors with time—
green, a newborn that dries

the mouth of the Sahara
but add salt and olive oil—

Mofongo! Tostones!
A bit of yellow grows

and your tongue screams
ambrosia!

Sweetness from the frying pan,
layered with meat becomes *piñón*—

lasagna of the tropics.
But wait!

When he is an old black man—

ODA AL PLÁTANO

Oh, fatuo conquistador
por qué la papa, con su piel de bebé sucio

con su forma tan banal e indigna
se pronunció comida esencial del mundo

debajo de tu nariz aguileña crecía
el verde, fálico, magnífico

¡plátano!
Piel de acero que exige un machete.

¿No viste su forma—
duro, macho y excitado?

Multitud de colores con el tiempo—
verde, un recién nacido que seca

la boca del Sahara.
pero ponle sal y aceite de oliva—

¡Mofongo! ¡Tostones!
Un poco de amarillo se asoma

y la lengua grita
¡Ambrosia!

Dulzura de la sartén
en capas con carne se convierte en piñón—

lasaña del trópico.
¡Espera!

Hasta que es un negro viejo—

softer, shriveled, and arrogant

basking in honey and oven steam—
he fills your mouth with Amazonian water.

más blando, arrugado, y arrogante

tomando el sol con vapor de horno—
llena tu boca con agua amazónica.

MACHETERO

He rests against his machete
for the third time
as the sugar cane burns.
A stench of molasses soot
fills the yellowed air
with acrid breath.
In cement and iron houses
fanning women curse—*¡Cabrón¡*
We can't hang out our clothes lines today.

Lifting his machete he
begins whacking
the razor-edged leaves
so soft and undulating
they lacerate his sun-burned chest.
He sings the accustomed and familiar prayer
—*Ay le lo lay, le lo le lo lay.*
Down the road to the town, the women
with cotton dresses and plastic sandals
accuse—*Con este calor y ese maldito infierno.*

At sundown he rests
his machete against
his naked back
black sweat covering his body.
Traffic silencing the cries of the *cañaveral*
the *alisio* winds lifting new sights and cleaner air—
with the last remaining egrets
he goes down the road to wherever...

The women hover
with resignation and exhausted faces
begin to close the iron gates.

EL MACHETERO

Apoyándose en su machete
por tercera vez
con la caña de azúcar quemando.
Un olor a hollín de melaza
se filtra en el aire amarillento
con el aliento agrio.
En casas de cemento e hierro,
mujeres abanicándose, lo maldicen—¡Cabrón!
Hoy no podemos colgar la ropa.

Levantando su machete
comenzó a golpear
hojas de filo de navaja
tan suaves y ondulantes
laceran su pecho tostado de sol.
Canta la acostumbrada y familiar oración,
—Ay le lo lay, le lo le lo lay.
En el camino a la ciudad, las mujeres
con vestidos de algodón y sandalias de plástico
lo acusan—*Con este calor y ese maldito infierno.*

Al caer el sol descansa
su machete contra
su espalda desnuda
el sudor negro tendido sobre su cuerpo.
El tráfico calla los gritos del cañaveral
y el alisio levanta una vista nueva y aire más limpio—
con las últimas garzas
regresa por el camino a donde sea que vaya...

Las mujeres acorraladas
con resignación y agotamiento en sus caras
comienzan a cerrar las puertas de hierro.

SAN JUAN'S NIGHT:
A DIALOGUE WITH THE ALISIO WIND

*June 24 marks the birthday of Saint John, Puerto Rico's
Patron Saint. The custom is to jump backwards three times
in a row into the ocean at midnight. This will bring good
fortune and will erase the past year.*

All is running madness
  —la noche de San Juan
to jump into the Atlantic
  —before the waves get mad.

The saints and Changó reigning
  —with candles burning air
to wash with turbid ocean
  —all foreboding cares.

The bongos loudly playing
  —*a ba catum banbo banbo é.*
The negro's hands are saying
  —they want to fly away!

The scantily dressed women
  —their breasts seething lust
with ocean and with laughter
  —under the eyes of men.

The night is hiding lovers
  —the sand accepts their thoughts.
They are making furious coitus
  —among the legs of drunks.

Our eyes are full of wonder
  —*la noche de San Juan.*
We jump the witching hour
  —and hope that all is well.

LA NOCHE DE SAN JUAN:
DIÁLOGO CON EL VIENTO ALISO

*Junio 24 marca el cumpleaños de San Juan Bautista,
Santo Patrón de Puerto Rico. La costumbre indica brincar
tres veces de espaldas al mar a la medianoche. Esto trae
suerte y borra el año pasado.*

Todo es locura
   —La noche de San Juan
para saltar en el Atlántico
   —antes que las olas embravecen.

Los santos y Changó reinan
   —velas queman el aire
pa' lavar con túrbido océano
   —de presentimientos que pesan.

Los bongos están tocando fuerte
   —*a ba catum banbo banbo é.*
Las manos del negro dicen
   —¡como les gustaría volar!

Las mujeres escasamente vestidas
   —sus senos embullen lujuria
con mar y con risa
   —bajo los ojos de los hombres.

La noche esconde amantes
   —arenas acceden sus pensamientos.
Ejecutan un coito furioso
   —entre las piernas de pordioseros.

Nuestros ojos llenos de anhelo.
   —*la noche de San Juan.*
Saltamos a la hora hechicera
   —y esperamos que todo salga bien.

PLAZA PALMER DE CAGUAS

Plaza afternoons of patent leather shoes
white socks and petticoats
running amuck, succumbing
to heat, sweat, and upbraided hair.

Ficus nitida—a looming monster
a quixotic protector—
stretches his branches
of green abandon
inviting
a billion black-purple
iridescences
with yellow quizzical eyes—
the Antillean grackle, *el chango.*

Below the avian noise
roots are
entangled maiden legs.
Motionless dancers
who welcome the climb of
lizards, *anolis*—
and small hands
who live, hide, and whisper
in its silken bark
who delight in cool darkness.

Scattered under the pool
of his vigilant shade
old men
in *guayaberas*, pleated pants,
fedoras of a different generation.
Dominoes at hand, they slam
the stained slab of old cement tables
with their eloquent palms full of wisdom.

PLAZA PALMER DE CAGUAS

Tardes de plaza en zapatos de charol
medias blancas y faldas
corriendo furiosamente, sucumbiendo
la trenza al calor, el sudor.

Ficus nitida—un enorme monstruo
protector quijotesco—
estira sus ramas
un abandono verde
invoca
a billones de un negro-púrpura
iridiscentes
con ojos amarillos burlones—
el grackle antillano, el chango.

Debajo del estruendo aviar
raíces son
enredadas piernas de soltera.
Bailarinas inmóviles
que acogen la subida de
lagartos, *anolis*—
y manos pequeñas
que viven, se esconden, y susurran
en su corteza de seda
deleitándose en la oscuridad fresca.

Dispersos bajo la alberca
de su sombra vigilante
los viejitos
en guayaberas, pantalones con pliegues,
fedoras de una generación diferente.
Dominó en la mano, golpean
viejas mesas de cemento teñido
con sus palmas elocuentes de conocimiento.

—Te lo dije maricón, la caja de dientes.—
A language all its own for the occasion
with rum in open vessels,
glasses that sweat of
Bacardí, Don Q, or *pitorro Cagüeño.*

Between the green and mildew
color
the flowers of the town—
dressed in cotton to
avert the heat—
shade themselves
with fans, lipstick, purses
murmuring
like kittens
their loves and their desires.

At six, exhaustion lifts
light breeze scatters
lizards
grackles
flowers
dominoes
as the massive green arms
sway
beckoning all to come again.

—Te lo dije maricón, la caja de dientes.—
Un lenguaje propio para la ocasión
con ron en recipientes abiertos,
vasos que sudan de
Bacardí, Don Q, o pitorro cagüeño.

Entre el verde y el moho
color
las flores de la ciudad—
en vestidos de algodón para
evitar el calor—
sombreándose
con abanicos, lápiz de labios, carteras
murmurando
como gatitas
sus amores y sus deseos.

A las seis, el agotamiento levanta
una brisita que dispersa
lagartos
changos
flores
fichas de dominó
mientras los masivos brazos verdes
se vaivean
invitando a que todos vengan de nuevo.

REMEMBERING THE TURABO

Looking through hot and dilapidated
classroom windows
decorated with the dewlap
of lizards
hoping to escape
on the white and blue streamers
of my Schwinn Tiger
to a world of imaginary waters
my river
the manly and ugly Turabo.
Half dead in thin mud
with thickets of tangled plants
that whispered tantalizing obscenities
to me, an eloping Catholic
in uniform, mentally undressing myself
for his element.
With timid tits I probed his breath—
my buttocks warming to his embrace.
Satiated in his water
mentally swimming
with phantomless fish of long ago.
The Turabo had testicles of catfish
caressing with kisses of gray and black tadpoles.
His green-brown arms
floating me away
free
from rulers, teachers, friends.
That river loved me
devoured me
and with slippery pebbles tickled
the soles of my bare feet
free in mind

Speaking at a Time — AMELIA DÍAZ ETTINGER

RECORDANDO EL TURABO

Mirando através de calientes y ruinosas
ventanas del aula
decoradas con la papada
de lagartos
con la esperanza de escapar
en las serpentinas blancas y azules
de mi Schwinn Tiger
a un mundo de aguas imaginarias
mi río
el varonil y deslucido Turabo.
Medio muerto en fango demacrado
con matorrales de plantas enredadas
que susurraba obscenidades tentadoras
para mí, una católica prófuga
en uniforme, mentalmente desnudándome
a su elemento.
Con tetillas tímidas probé su aliento—
mis nalgas calentándose a su abrazo.
Saciada en su agua
nadando mentalmente
con peces espectros de antaño.
El Turabo tenía testículos de bagre
y acariciaba con besos grises y negros
de renacuajos.
Sus brazos verde-marrón
me flotaba
libre
de reglas, maestros, amigos.
Ese río me amaba
me devoraba
con piedritas resbaladizas me cosquilleaba
las plantas de mis pies descalzos
libre en mente

from perennial Buster Browns.
Then, as all secret lovers do,
deposited me
soiled with algae
back to books, lectures, uniform
virginal.

de perennes *Buster Browns*.
Entonces, como todos los amantes secretos
me depositaba
manchada con algas
de regreso a libros, lecciones, uniforme
virginal.

EL YUNQUE

Sometimes I long to be alone
in a humid room that smells of moths and rotting leaves
where yellow light filters through the sweat of plants
and embraces me with windless arms—
so unlike the arms of open spaces—
where I can hear the voices of the dead:
—*Yunque, Huracán...Borinquén*

I want to be in this shadowed room
where canopy and moss-like dirt
share secrets with the senses
where dew collects on dwarfed trees
where my voice could be thunder
of a tree frog chorus:
—*¡Coquí, coquí, coquí!*

Then my dreams could be the eyes of lizards
Anolis occultus, Anolis evermanni, Anolis roosevelti
my gender the crimson crown of the Puerto Rican parrot
Amazona vittata
flying unencumbered to copulate among the green.

EL YUNQUE

A veces anhelo estar sola
en un cuarto húmedo que huele a polilla y hojas podridas
donde la luz amarillenta se filtra con el sudor de las plantas
y te abraza con brazos sin viento—
tan diferentes a los brazos de espacios abiertos—
Donde puedo escuchar las voces de los muertos:
—*Yunque, Huracán...Borinquén*

Quiero estar en esa sala de sombra
donde techo verde y musgo sucio
comparte secretos con los sentidos
donde el rocío se acumula en árboles enanos
donde mi voz podría ser el trueno
de un coro de ranitas:
—*¡Coquí, coquí, coquí!*

Entonces mis sueños podrían ser los ojos de los lagartijos
Anolis occultus, Anolis evermanni, Anolis roosevelti
mi sexo la corona escarlata de la cotorra puertorriqueña
Amazona vittata
volando sin compromiso a copular entre lo verde.

SPEAKING AT A TIME

Webster open on her lap
my daughter turns
her pale blue eyes to me.
She asks, *What is heritage?*
And waits for an answer that has to reach
three thousand miles to say:

A building of cement by the Caguas Plaza
full—
of aunts and uncles, *tíos y tías*
all talking at the same time—
advice, admonitions, lectures on virginity.
While *café con leche* streams in *la cocina*
grandfather, *abuelo*, snores, his octogenarian siesta
filling the streets with majestic bellowing
from three stories above so a pedestrian shouts
—*¡Dios mío, como ronca ese pobre diablo!*

It is roasting coffee beans
at three o'clock from *La Central*
the fragrance of a pregnant town
Caguas—
who aches with traffic
going the wrong way on a one way street
car jams and taxis that stop
to make words of love to a woman with big hips
the patience of pedestrians
clearing the way for fast cars
even faster buses
el pisicorre on sidewalks.

It is a tolerance and generosity for street urchins
with swollen bellies who lie and steal and wish
money given freely between people.

HABLANDO A LA VEZ

Con Webster abierto en su regazo
mi hija fija
sus ojos azul-claro en mí.
Pregunta, ¿Qué es herencia?
Y espera una respuesta
que tiene que llegar a
tres mil millas para decir:

Un edificio de cemento en la Plaza de Caguas
repleto—
de tíos y tías
hablando al mismo tiempo—
consejos, advertencias, lecciones sobre la virginidad.
Mientras que el café con leche humea en la cocina
abuelo, sueña su siesta octogenaria
llenando la calle con un roncado majestuoso
 desde tres pisos de altura, que hacen gritar a un peatón
—¡Dios mío, como ronca ese pobre diablo!

Es café tostado
a las tres de la tarde en La Central
la fragancia de un pueblo embarazado
Caguas—
que sufre por un tráfico
que van por el sentido contrario
tapones y taxis que se detienen
para hacer palabras de amor a una mujer con caderas grandes
es la paciencia de peatones
saltando del camino para los coches rápidos
y aún más para guaguas
el pisicorre en las aceras.

Es tolerancia y generosidad para los niños de las calles
con vientres hinchados que mienten roban y anhelan
dinero dado libremente entre la gente.

My daughter, it is a swarm of people in uniforms
filling Benitez and Loiza Streets
as the factory empties and schools let out
girls in the public-plaid nervously eyeing
the white and khaki of indifferent "private" boys
of men with badges and *macanas* searching
the roundness underneath white aprons
women rushing to get home to other work
a green and red disorder
of mangoes in pick-up trucks or *el mercado*
—*Mangó fresquito a diez chavo*, the loudspeaker
hidden in the earthy odor of tubers
—*¡Ñame, yautía, papas,...tó barato!*
an explosion of burlap filled
with *habichuelas, maíz*, and sorrow.

It is music against music, from radios
stores, houses, cars, and the boys on the sidewalk
playing salsa, merengue, rumba, boleros, and rock
bongos en la plaza,
and urbanizations, tight muscled men banging
their palms to the rhythm of dreams.
Heritage is politics shouted from moving vans
in neckties or guayaberas and orthodontic smiles:
—*Vote por la Estadidad* (blue and white)
—*Vote por los Populares* (red and white)
—*Vote por la Independencia* (white and hope).

It is Catholicism and *Santerismo*
Vatican saints dressed in velvet at the cathedral
a wooden African god in your neighbor's yard
a Latin rosary prayed in living-rooms
while holy water and bay alcohol sprinkle
the bed of a dying man
or the shoulders of a new *señorita*.
It is a celebration of food and sex and death
in the *barrio, boticario*, and *colmados*.

Mi hija, es un hervidero de gente en uniformes
llenando las calles de Benítez y de Loíza
vaciándose las fábricas y las escuelas abren las puertas
las niñas en el público-a cuadros mirando nerviosamente
el blanco y el caqui de los niños "privados" indiferentes
de los hombres con escudos y macanas ojeando
la redondez debajo de delantales blancos
mujeres corriendo a casa a otro trabajo
un trastorno verde y rojo
de mangos en camionetas o del mercado
—*Mango fresquito a diez chavos*, el altavoz
escondido en el aroma a tierra de tubérculos
—*¡Ñame, yautía, papas,...to' barato!*
una explosión de arpillera llena de
habichuelas, maíz, y tristeza.

Es música contra música, de las radios
tiendas, casas, coches, y los chicos en la acera
tocando salsa, merengue, rumba, boleros y rock
bongos en la plaza,
y las urbanizaciones, hombres musculosos golpeando
sus palmas al ritmo de los sueños.
Herencia es política gritada desde camiones
en corbata o guayaberas y con sonrisas ortodóntas:
—Vote Por La Estadidad (azul y blanco)
—Vote Por los Populares (rojo y blanco)
—Vote Por La Independencia (blanco y esperanza)

Es catolicismo y santería
santos del Vaticano vestidos de terciopelo en la catedral
un dios africano de madera en el patio del vecino
un rosario rezado en latín en la sala
mientras que agua santa y alcohol con malagueta rocía
la cama de un hombre moribundo
o los hombros de una nueva señorita.
Es una celebración de comida de sexo y de muerte
en el barrio, boticario, y colmados.

Hot streams of semen, olive oil, garlic, and incense
all speaking at a time to music
bongos, maracas, y güiros, and a badly spoken *español*
—*Ta' ca' detrá, chico.*
It is laughter and tears and strife.
It is the siren at six o'clock
sending people home
to begin the night
as the trade wind picks up
and mingles with more cars and more traffic
voicing its concern with the chorus of tree frogs:
—*Coquí, coquí, coquí, coquí*
—*¿De dónde vienes?*
—*¿Pá' dónde vas?*

It is Sundays at the horse races
holding tightly to the green paper
or eating *pastelillos* on Luquillo Beach
while children learn to swim
and older sisters learn to make love
and matrons run to the cemetery
to bring flowers to the other loves.

It is the warmth of a familiar tongue
with *Tío Carlos, Tití Ligia, Gisela, Marisol*
who bring rum, *tembleque,* blood sausage
in the long history behind their eyes.
It is, in fact, what you, my daughter, *mi hija*
didn't inherit.

Corrientes de semen caliente, aceite de oliva, ajo, e incienso
todos hablando a la vez con la música
bongos, maracas, güiros, y español *malhablao*
—'Ta 'ca detrá', chico.
Es la risa y las lágrimas y la lucha.
Es la sirena de las seis
mandado gente a casa
para comenzar la noche
mientras el alisio alza
y se mezcla con más coches y más tráfico
expresando su preocupación con el coro de ranitas:
—Coquí, coquí, coquí, coquí
—¿De dónde vienes?
—¿Pa' dónde vas?

Es domingos en las carreras de caballos
sosteniendo firmemente el papel verde
o comiendo pastelillos en la playa de Luquillo
mientras los niños aprenden a nadar
las hermanas mayores aprenden hacer el amor
y las matronas corren al cementerio
para llevar flores a otros amores.

Es el calor de una lengua familiar
con Tío Carlos, Tití Ligia, Gisela, Marisol
que traen ron, tembleque, morcilla
es la larga historia que traen detrás de sus ojos.
De hecho, es lo que, tú, mi hija, *mihja'*
no heredaste.

PART 2 | PARTE 2

EXILE

Hour upon hour spent in this cell
thinking of *tamarindos* and *guayabas*
the taste of sun within my throat.

Hour upon hour, this thirst won't perish.
Words that sound of coconut water
that smell of ocean and mulattoes

now silent.
This thirst grows like grime
hour upon hour reliving

the Sunday dresses in the *iglesia*
my uncles in *guayaberas* playing *dominó*
the taste of politics in the public bus

waves of skin in the *mercado*
mangó, guineos, and sacks of *habichuelas.*
Hour upon hour spent in this cell

thinking of *tamarindos* and *guayabas*
the taste of sun
within my throat.

EXILIO

Hora tras hora en esta célula
pensando en tamarindos y guayabas
con sabor a sol en mi garganta.

Hora tras hora, la sed no sucumbe.
Palabras que suenan a agua de coco
con olor a océano y mulatos

ahora en silencio.
Esta sed que crece como la suciedad
hora tras hora reviviendo

los vestidos de domingo en la iglesia
mis tíos en guayaberas jugando dominó,
el sabor a política en la guagua pública

olas de piel en el mercado
mangó, guineos, y sacos de habichuelas.
Hora tras hora pasándola en esta celda

pensando en tamarindos y guayabas
sabor a sol
dentro de mi garganta.

THE ROOSTER CALLS THREE TIMES

Being Puerto Rican is no fucking easy.
It is a stigma like the *mancha de plátano*
or the charlatan's saint bleeding hands.
It is starch, sea water, fish, breeze
estuary, and desert—
all fighting to command
no one taking charge.

It is smelling the Mediterranean
in Caribbean sugar cane and rum
having Castile's noble castles made
of Yoruba drums
masking a noble *vejigante*
with sadistic dreams.

We scratch the skin, the soil, the flag, and ask
Who are we?
Who the hell are we?
Yet answer with what we are not:
—My grandfather not black but lilac
—My mother from Madrid, Galicia, Barcelona
—My brother incarnation of *Babaluaye*.

Even our tongue betrays us—
an Anglo-Castilian locomotive
that purrs like a jackhammer
in anguish to expose
what holds our soil.
Congo? Borinquén? Iberia?—

we embrace and glorify all three:
singing our drums, reciting Quixotic verses

EL GALLO LLAMA TRES VECES

Ser puertorriqueña no es joder fácil.
Es un estigma como la mancha de plátano
o las manos sangrantes del charlatán santo.
Se trata de almidón, agua de mar, peces, brisa
estuario, y desierto—
todos combatiendo a mandar
nadie haciéndose cargo.

Es olor a mediterráneo
en la caña de azúcar caribeña y ron
tener nobles castillos de Castilla hechos
de tambores de Yoruba
enmascarando a un vejigante noble
con sueños sádicos.

Nos rascamos la piel, la tierra, la bandera, y preguntamos
¿Quiénes somos?
¿Quién carajo somos?
Sin embargo, respondemos con lo que no somos:
—Mi abuelo no era negro pero lila.
—Mi madre de Madrid, Galicia, Barcelona
—Mi hermano encarnación de Babaluaye.

Hasta nuestra lengua nos traiciona—
una locomotora anglo-castellana
que ronronea como un martillo neumático
en la angustia de exponer
que mantiene nuestro suelo.
¿Congo? ¿Borinquén ¿Iberia?—

abrazamos y glorificamos a los tres:
cantando nuestros tambores, recitando versos quijotescos

yearning from our Taino hammocks.
Alisio wind to our backs, we call—
Elegguá, Youcahu, Jesús... until midnight,

Then, like Peter, we deny all three.

mientras añoramos desde hamacas taínas.
El Alisio a nuestras espaldas convocamos—
Elegguá, Youcahu, Jesús... hasta la medianoche,

Entonces, como Pedro, negamos a los tres.

PUERTO RICAN IN OREGON

I am these memories embedded in my cells—
lipids, ions that continually shed
yet stay constant.

I am this town—Caguas—
hot and humid like my loins
where the air is sipped
like coffee at three in the afternoon.

These mind-memory cells, a honeycomb
of dirty streets buzzing with pedestrians
cars without mufflers, radios, shouts, children
learning the rhythm of a bolero, salsa, and colonization.

I am the memory of elegant cement
in front of a dying plaza
a girl with thin bones waltzing
to her internal melancholy.
I am a lecture on virginity
a school uniform starched rigidly
a prisoner of Catholicism
and a gambling genteel father.

I am his voice and hands
the legacy of coffee and tobacco
the arrogance of Spain
in a world that whistles Africa
tribal drums, sweat, and machetes
a world that sinks and floats in my synaptic magma.

Now I look through my round window—
Mount Emily's pachydermic figure

PUERTORRIQUEÑA EN OREGÓN

Soy estas memorias incrustadas en mis células—
lípidos, iones que se desprenden continuamente
y sin embargo se mantienen constantes.

Soy este pueblo—Caguas—
caliente y húmedo como mis muslos
donde el aire se bebe
como el café a las tres de la tarde.

Estas células-memoria, un panal de abejas
de calles sucias repletas de peatones
coches sin silenciadores, radios, gritos, niños
aprendiendo el ritmo de bolero, salsa, y colonización.

Yo soy el recuerdo de cemento elegante
frente a una plaza moribunda
una chica con huesos delgados bailando un vals
de melancolía interna.
Soy una lección en virginidad
un uniforme almidonado rígidamente
prisionera católica
y un tierno padre jugador de casino.

Yo soy su voz y sus manos
el legado de café y tabaco
la arrogancia de España
en un mundo que silba África,
tambores tribales, sudor, y machetes
un mundo que se hunde y flota en mi magma sináptica.

Ahora miro por mi ventana redonda—
a la paquidérmica montaña Emily

buttressing against my internal cordillera.
I drink Scotch instead of Rum
play cribbage not dominoes.

I am this woman stepping with the wrong rhythm
in streets so empty they echo like holocaust
after six, under a sky that sighs
gray to country western songs
answering to "Mother" or "Mom"
not *mamá*, never *mamita*.

I am this cold politeness
that carries well under this northern sun
a serious dress and quiet shoes
that hide a song that smells fertile
tapping and orchestrating somnolent
in a skin that feels like termites.

acorralada en contra de mi Cordillera interna.
Yo bebo whisky en vez de ron
juego naipes no dominó.

Yo soy esa mujer caminando con un ritmo equivocado
en calles tan vacías que resuenan a holocausto
después de las seis, bajo un cielo que suspira
canciones grises de *country western*,
respondiendo a "*mother*" o "*mom*"
No a mamá, nunca a mamita.

Soy esta cortesía fría
que va bien bajo este sol norteño
un vestido sobrio y zapatos silenciosos
que ocultan una canción que huele fértil
tocando y orquestando somnolienta
en una piel que se siente como termitas.

NIGHTS IN OREGON

It is worse at night
when the images no longer stand behind my eyes
and Anglo words can no longer stifle my cries.
If from my pillow the perfume from my shoulder floats
to me
I see women in black
knitting
conversing
cross-stitching
from balcony
to balcony
hysterical laughter
from the fabrics in their hands.

It is worse at night
when a forgotten radio hints
in a consonant language words of passion
and loss.
Drums and a ten string guitar—*el cuatro*
fill my mouth
with need
for music that tastes of rum and cigar
of a lost *barrio*
with young girls
with budding breasts
and yearning hearts.

Yes, it is worse at night
when a rare aroma from a nocturnal kitchen
breezes
in
a constellation of people
dances

NOCHES EN OREGÓN

Es peor en la noche
cuando las imágenes ya no están detrás de mis ojos
y las palabras inglesas ya no pueden reprimir mis gritos.
Y si de mi almohada el perfume de mi hombro flota
a mí
veo mujeres en negro
tejiendo
conversando
punto de cruz
de balcón
a balcón
risa histérica
de las telas en sus manos.

Es peor en la noche
cuando un olvidado radio recuerda
en palabras llenas de consonantes palabras de pasión
y pérdida.
Tambores y una guitarra de diez cuerdas—el cuatro
llena mi boca
con necesidad
de la música con sabor a ron y tabaco
de un barrio perdido
con niñas
de pechos en ciernes
y anhelo en sus corazones.

Sí, es peor en la noche
cuando un raro aroma de una cocina nocturna
se cuela
adentro
una constelación de personas
danzan

into my room
laughter and sweat mingle with
the illusion of *bocadillos*.

It is worst of all on a warm and humid night
with the scent of sex and dripping wax.
Then, the dancers converge around my bed
their voices palpable in moonlight
waiting for the darkness in me
to engulf them.

en mi habitación
risa y sudor se mezclan con
bocadillos ilusorios.

Lo peor de todo es en una noche cálida y húmeda
con olor a sexo y cera derretida.
Entonces, los danzantes convergen alrededor de mi cama
sus voces palpables a la luz de la luna
esperando que mi oscuridad
los envuelva.

HALF OF ME

Half of me stands looking
looking for the cinnamon soul intact.
Standing, I want to see myself—
Hablando claro y florido.
Ay, cuántos años hubiese
en besos dar.
De mi completa, perfecta,
exuberante.

No. I stand an aging woman
in Levis, fumbling for words
elusive, passive
monument to adaptability
metamorphosed
wanting to ask:
—¿Te acuerdas de mi?
Con el sexo virginal suspirando.
Corriendo por el cementerio
de la infancia.

Where is the pain and the sin?
Maybe it was a sin to leave?
The price was half of me.
My lines lose their fluency
just like my lost virginity.
Now, I try to remember sin
before it kissed pain.
A stroll in salty air?
It is just a memory
without freedom.

Now, I wish to expand
my lungs in ecstasy
returning barefoot

MI MITAD

Una parte de mi me mira
buscando el alma canela intacta.
Parada, quiero verme—
Hablando claro y florido.
Ay, cuántos años hubiese
en besos dar.
De mi completa, perfecta,
exuberante.

No. Soy una mujer envejeciendo
en *Levis*, con palabras rotas
elusiva, pasiva
un monumento a la adaptabilidad
metamorfoseada
esperando a preguntar:
—*¿Te acuerdas de mi?*
Con el sexo virginal suspirando.
Corriendo por el cementerio
de la infancia.

¿Dónde está el dolor y el pecado?
¿Tal vez el pecado fue irme?
El precio es la mitad de mi.
Con versos mustios sin elocuencia,
como la pérdida virginal.
Ahora, trato de recordar el pecado
antes de besar el dolor.
¿Una caminata en aire salitre?
Es solo una memoria
sin libertad.

Ahora, quiero expandir
mis pulmones en éxtasis
regresando descalza

with black hair
black as the dreams of a lizard.
Then, I scream because I have value!
I have value!
Like my country has value.

Half of me stands dying these years
with yearnings for sights not seen
waiting to love a present or a future
with eyes firmly planted on days gone
of childhood memories
dreaming of men that never were
of roller-skates and velvet dresses
of coconut candy
de....

con el cabello negro
negro como un sueño de lagarto.
¡Entonces, grito porque valgo!
¡Valgo!
Como la patria vale.

Una parte de mi muere en estos años
con anhelos de vistas que ya existen
esperando amar un presente o un futuro
con ojos plantados firmemente en días desaparecidos
de memorias infantiles
soñando con hombres que nunca fueron
de patines y trajes de terciopelo
de dulces de coco
de...

RELATIVE LIGHT

Here it is again, that light—

familiar and foreign—
that enters my Oregon window
smelling of Jackie's tea and British cakes
of my aunt's embroidery
her quiet conversations

light that sings like a mountain—
Cascade or *Cordillera*—
that scatters air like *colibrí* or magpie.
It is my son's light as he ponders his new found life
light of my dead father's appraising eyes.

Here it is again, the light

that feeds on the worms of childhood
and waltzes the dust particles of age
the light that enters with the warmth
of quiet perfume
wrapped in my beautiful Mayra's hair
tasting of ancient summers balancing on swings.

This is the light that wraps time
in my daughter's laughter
the texture of river escapades and first kisses
a brilliance gentle as a thought
that rouses a volcano.

LUZ FAMILIAR

Aquí está otra vez, esa luz—

familiar y forastera—
que entra por mi ventana de Oregón
que huele al té y los pasteles británicos de Jackie,
del bordado de mi tía
sus conversaciones calladas

luz que canta como una montaña—
Cascade o Cordillera—
que dispersa aire como colibrí o *magpie.*
Es la luz de mi hijo sopesando su vida nueva
luz evaluadora de los ojos de mi padre muerto.

Aquí está otra vez, la luz

que se alimenta de los gusanos de la infancia
y valse las partículas de polvo de los años
esta luz que entra con el calor
de perfume tranquilo
envuelto en el cabello de mi bella Mayra
que sabe a veranos de antaño balanceando en columpios.

Esta luz que envuelve el tiempo
en la risa de mi hija
la textura de escapadas a ríos y los primeros besos
un brillo apacible como un pensamiento
que despierta un volcán.

THE UNTRANSLATED

Words locked in fresh cement
hardening.

They can't float or swim
find a form or dance.

Limited to contemplate
without a simple *te quiero*

never flying or being heard.
Do I sound like myself in this Anglo world?

Yo amo la vida, la patria...
Words mired in consonants like poison

at the lintel of my conscience—
inert

aghast—
mohosas, inertes, insaciables.

Rusting at weather's travel
time

hiding them even from my own desires.

PART 3 | PARTE 3

DON PABLO NERUDA

Don Pablo!
As a god I call on you.
Come!
Erect an ode to the other smaller Guatemala—
rectangular island
suckling pig.
Help me!
Don
god
Pablo
Neruda
with the sharpness of your pen.
Return, be a man of blood—
poet
saint
god.
My people die
without Betances' voice.
Conduct in rhythm
a concert with Doña Lola
Lloréns Torres
and the Cagüeño Gautier.
Come!
Write another ode to the small
undernourished
disdained
prostituted earth
that nurses with flaccid
tits
the barbarian Northerners
with avarice and lust.

Don Pablo! Pablo! Mi Pablo!
I call upon you as a prayer

DON PABLO NERUDA

¡Don Pablo!
Como a un dios te llamo.
¡Ven!
Construye una oda a la otra más pequeña Guatemala—
isla rectangular
puerquito de teta.
¡Ayudame!
Don
dios
Pablo
Neruda
con tu afilada pluma.
Regresa, un hombre de sangre—
poeta
santo
dios.
Mi gente muere
sin la voz de Betances.
Conduce en ritmo
un concierto con Doña Lola
Lloréns Torres
el cagüeño Gautier.
¡Ven!
Escribe otra oda a la pequeña
malnutrida
desdeñada
tierra prostituida
que mama con flácidas
tetas
a los bárbaros norteños
con avaricia y lujuria.

¡Don Pablo! ¡Pablo! ¡Mi Pablo!
Te invoco como oración

to the Immaculate Conception
white serious matron
of this red soil—
soil transversed like spears
by the Cordillera and foreigners
who get lost—
this damned earth
that dines black blood
earth that is not earth
but burial territory
purgatory of souls
that float in limbo
with open eyes.

You
who come from such a long seacoast
so much fertile sand
who carry the shield of the bard
habla
write
scream
the music of this other island
that cries of violent deaths
in chaotic streets
of hands that want
cocaine, money
of towns that smell
of water-bread
hot plantains
tubers
y dulce de leche.

Tell me!
Great god of words—
what will the children hear
of their Occidental beauty

Speaking at a Time — AMELIA DÍAZ ETTINGER

a la Inmaculada Concepción
patrona blanca y seria
de esta tierra roja—
tierra atravesada como lanza
por Cordillera y extranjeros
que se pierden—
esta tierra maldita
que come la sangre negra
tierra que no es tierra
pero cementerio
purgatorio de almas
que flotan en limbo
con ojos abiertos.

Tú
que vienes de esa costa larga
de fértiles arenas
que llevas el escudo del bardo
habla
escribe
grita
la música de esta otra isla
que llora de muertes violentas
en calles caóticas
de manos que quieren
la cocaína, el dinero
de pueblos que huelen
a pan de agua
plátanos calientes
tubérculos
y dulce de leche.

¡Dime!
Gran dios de letras—
¿qué oirán los niños
de la belleza occidental

tropical
quasi equatorial
of the defunct roasting of coffee
and the ghost of sugar cane?
What about El Yunque
hill
mountain
continent
navigating eye of the Tainos
and indomitable plants
and rebels and rebellions?

tropical
cuasi-equatorial
del difunto café tostado
y el fantasma de la caña de azúcar?
¿Y qué del Yunque
monte
montaña
continente
el ojo navegante del Taíno
y de plantas indomables
rebeldes y rebeliones?

A POEM FOR LORCA

I sat by the fountain
when my hair was young
waiting for fortune
or a man
to take me away.
When he came
with a lily in his hand
and a dryness on his lips
from so much loving
or maybe longing—
a Granadian soul—
I gave him nothing.

And since
then, I have found
moon and man
and in that desert
returned to that fountain
to find his lily
as always—
white, radiant
with his blood.
I have taken the lily to bed
and in our solitude we pray.
She gives me his water
and still
I give him nothing.

UN POEMA PARA LORCA

Me senté por la fuente
cuando mi cabello era joven
esperando fortuna
o un hombre
que me llevara lejos.
Cuando él vino
con un lirio en su mano
y una aridez en los labios
de tanto amar
o tal vez anhelar—
un alma granadina—
y no le di nada.

Desde entonces
encontré
luna y hombre
y en su desierto
regresé a su fuente
para encontrar su lirio
como siempre—
blanca, resplandeciente
con su sangre.
Me he llevado el lirio a la cama
y en nuestra soledad oramos.
Ella me da su agua
y todavía
a él no le doy nada.

ESPERANZA PÉREZ YOUR NAME IS HOPE

In restlessness you return
Esperanza
to sew
circles of cloth
vestiges of my family.
Your two-tone hands
that make *arroz con pollo*
and turn our beds at night
move
fabric—
a manta ray of color
on your succulent lap
a lap for a motherless girl
a lap without your own
children.

Where was your son
when you told me of your skin?
A curse, you said, to be black
but your skin smelled of coconut
and milk and you.
The needle bites the cloth
and on your lips
a quiet prayer trembles
at the hour your door is closed
and candles burn
for *Santa Bárbara* and *Changó*.
—*A bayombe bombé*
batombé
a yombe, yombe, bombé.
A distant drum marks the rhythm
in your wily hand
as the thread makes the circles grow.

ESPERANZA PÉREZ NO SOLO ES TU NOMBRE

En la inquietud tú regresas
Esperanza
a coser
círculos de tela
vestigios de mi familia.
Tus manos de dos colores
que hacen arroz con pollo
y las camas por la noche
mueven
tela—
una mantarraya de colores
en tu falda suculenta
falda para una niña sin madre
falda sin tus propios
hijos.

¿Dónde estaba tu hijo
cuando hablamos de tu piel?
Una maldición, dijiste, ser negra
pero tu piel olía a coco
y leche y a ti.
La aguja muerde la tela
y en tus labios
una oración silenciosa tiembla
a la hora en que tu puerta cierra
y las velas se encienden
para Santa Bárbara y Changó
—*A bayombe bombé*
batombé
a yombe, yombe, bombé.
Un tambor distante marca el ritmo
de tu mano diestra
mientras el hilo hace que los círculos crezcan.

TO MY COUSIN

Long before beauty or men came to matter
you and I held hands—
our frenzied legs running in surf
our laughter rising above the waves
like bubbles on the white foam.
Our hands entangled
tightly
to jump
landing soundlessly in the warm and green water.
I kissed your cheek, you combed my hair
snarled with sands and shells.
Tired, we let our bodies lie to warm
against the blue and cloudy skies—
cumulus rearranging in front of our eyes:
"Look! An elephant," I said.
"No! A cockroach," you responded,
sending more resounding laughter.
How I miss your golden air!
Quenching our thirst
we drank coconut water
our rounded fingertips barely touching.

A MI PRIMA

Antes que la belleza o los hombres hablarán
tú y yo tomadas de la mano—
nuestras loquillas piernas corriendo al mar
nuestra risa sobre las olas
como burbujas flotando sobre la espuma blanca.
Nuestras manos enredadas
sólidamente
para saltar
aterrizando silenciosamente en la agua cálida y verde.
Besé tu mejilla, y tú me peinaste
enredo de arena y concha.
Cansadas , dejamos que nuestros cuerpos se calentaran
contra un cielo azul nublado—
cúmulos frente a nuestros ojos se tornaban:
—Mira un elefante, yo te dije.
 —¡No Una cucaracha!, tú respondiste,
 creando otra ola de risotadas.
¡Cómo extraño tu aire de oro!
Saciando nuestra sed
mientras bebíamos agua de coco
nuestros dedos redonditos apenas tocando.

SUNDAY AT THE RACES

for my father

Sunday mornings always come the same
a piece of green showing
out of your pocket.

"Hurry to the car," you say
adrenaline burning
the swollen veins, your blotched forehead.

And thus we go.

Your thick and sometimes gentle hands
a strong fast grip, as if it is a promise
they are holding.
"This time for sure!"

Ice cream to appease me
at your side
while the radio blasts:
número seis, Capistrano, Ángel Cordero—
a hundred and six pounds—
a sure winner.

"You bet he is!" You tap the wheel.
I hide in the revolting stickiness
with hot vinyl against my sweating legs.

You push me past the revolving doors
losing ourselves in the mass
of bodies holding tightly to their smiles.

"Hurry, it is time." The words muddle
as the loudspeaker shouts
A sure winner!

DOMINGOS EN EL HIPÓDROMO

para Papi

Los domingos siempre empiezan iguales
un pedazo de papel verde
saliendo de tu bolsillo.

—Apúrate al carro, tú dices
adrenalina quemando
las venas hinchadas, de tu manchada frente.

Y así nos vamos.

Tus gruesas y a veces gentiles manos
una garra fuerte, como si fuera una promesa
lo que sostienen.
—¡Esta vez de seguro!

Mantecado para apaciguarme
a tu lado
mientras la radio grita:
Número seis, Capistrano, Ángel Cordero—
ciento seis libras—
un ganador seguro.

—¡Apuesto que sí! Tú golpeas el volante.
Yo invisible en la pegajosidad asqueante
del vinilo caliente en contra de mis piernas sudantes.

Me empujas por las puertas giratorias
perdiéndonos en las masas de cuerpos
sosteniendo firmemente las sonrisas.

—¡Apúrate, ya es tiempo! Las palabras se enredan
mientras el altoparlante grita
¡Un seguro ganador!

You bet he is!
You bet he is!
You bet.
You bet.

I pray as I see you kiss the green paper.
The gates open
dust lifts over a gaping crowd.
Capistrano!
Capistrano!
your voice a clenched fist
a stream of sweat
muscles and promises.

Your arms wave above my head.
I dare not move, might your luck be turned.
I dare not see the flashing colors
the man in red.

Thick and sometimes gentle hands
a strong fast grip against the rail—
a promise is descending.

The dust has settled one more time
lifting only the paper from your hand
your thick and lifeless hands
resting gently on my shoulders.

¡Apuesto que sí!
¡Apuesto que sí!
Apuesto.
Apuestas.

Yo ruego mientras te veo besar el papel verde.
Las puertas abren
el polvo se levanta sobre una muchedumbre boquiabierta.
¡Capistrano!
¡Capistrano!
tu voz un puño cerrado
un riachuelo de sudor
músculos y promesas.

Tus brazos agitando sobre mi cabeza.
Con miedo de moverme, que no cambie tu suerte.
Miedo de ver los colores relampagueantes
el hombre en rojo.

Gruesas y a veces gentiles manos
un puño aterrado a la cerca—
una promesa desciende.

El polvo se a sienta otra vez
levantando sólo el papel de tus manos
tus gruesas y muertas manos
reposan gentilmente en mis hombros.

THE HATSTAND OR THE STRANGE MEN?

Who were those *campesinos*
who came to visit but never passed the anteroom?
Hats in hand like steering wheels
polished, dead old shoes
skins darkened by sweat and circumstance
their cologne—earth, manhood, a hint of Brillantine.

The *campesinos'* hats never perched on the hatstand.
My uncle's hats, happy family of fat brown birds,
hung lightly there—
accustomed to dispense comfort, words,
money, maybe destiny
from human discomforts.

Alone in the parlor, "the anteroom," as it was called,
the men waited
and the hatstand stood:
dark mahogany arms from another century
mirror turned upwards ever so slightly
—an aristocratic eye—

tall thin aloofness hard and uninviting—
a blind glass eye to those *campesinos* who smelled of earth.
So many came and in silence waited—
the hatstand their sole companion
wooden witness to many wants.
Was it money, law, hope?
The hatstand never gave an answer.

¿EL PERCHERO O LOS EXTRAÑOS?

¿Quiénes eran esos campesinos
que venían a visitar, pero nunca pasaron de la antesala?
Sombreros en mano como volantes de un carro
con zapatos pulidos pero muertos
con pieles oscurecidas por el sudor y las circunstancias
su colonia—tierra, virilidad, y un toque de brillantina.

Los sombreros de los hombres nunca descansaron sobre
    el perchero.
Los de mis tíos, una familia feliz de pájaros gordos, marrones,
colgando a la ligera—
acostumbrados a repartir consuelos, palabras,
dinero, tal vez destino
de las molestias humanas.

A solas en la antesala
los hombres esperaban
y el perchero en pie:
brazos de caoba oscura de otro siglo
espejo dirigido brevemente hacia arriba
—un ojo aristocrático—

alto, delgado, indiferente, dura madera desdeñante—
un ojo de cristal ciego a aquellos campesinos que olían a tierra.
tantos vinieron y esperaron en silencio—
el perchero su único compañero
testigo de madera a sus anhelos.
¿Era dinero, ley, esperanza?
El perchero nunca dio respuesta.

TURKEY SANDWICH

Caribe Hilton Lobby, 1965

I'm waiting
for
maybe
a midnight snack, as my Papi called it
surrounded by one or two decrepit tourists
"Too early for bed, too late to care," the tourist motto.
Never afraid nor truly lonely
a pretty girl dressed well, to be sure,
no one would think me a lesser child.

Close to five in the morning
he pushes open the casino doors
cold humid air exhales putrid with cigars.
His lustrous smile above
the tuxedo, the gap between his teeth
so familiar and alien—
in his hands the turkey sandwich—
pale white meat that tastes of regret
and his affection

and affliction—
a morsel of fear in my Papi's hands.
Leaning my head on his shoulder
I devour all of it as we drive home
he smelling of blackjack
a smell stronger than his cologne, Old Spice
wishing
for
maybe.

SANDWICH DE PAVO

Vestíbulo del Caribe Hilton, 1965

Yo esperando
para
tal vez
una merienda de medianoche, como la llama Papi
rodeada de turistas decrépitos
—Muy temprano para dormir, muy tarde para importar,
    el lema turístico.
Sin miedo o realmente sola
linda niña bien vestida, para cerciorarse,
nadie me confundiría con una niña de menos.

Casi las cinco de la madrugada
cuando él abre las puertas del casino
un aire frío exhala putrefacto a cigarros.
Su lustrosa sonrisa sobre
el esmoquin, el huequito entre sus dientes
tan familiar y tan ajeno—
en sus manos un sándwich de pavo—
carne blanca que sabe a remordimiento
a su afecto

y aflicción—
un bocadillo de miedo en las manos de Papi.
Con mi cabeza inclinada en sus hombros
lo devoro en marcha a casa
él huele a veintiuna
olor que se aferra más fuerte que su colonia, *Old Spice*
esperando
para
tal vez.

SPEAKING AT A TIME
HABLANDO A LA VEZ

GLOSSARY

Ángel Cordero: famous Puerto Rican jockey, inducted to the United States Racing Hall of Fame

Anolis: genus of the fourteen species of iguanian lizards endemic to Puerto Rico

Ay, le, lo, lay: a common refrain used in poetry and song, it identifies a jíbaro (a countryman)

Babaluaye: also spelled Babalú-Ayé, is an Orisha from Santeria, he is associated with healing

Benítez: José Gautier Benítez, beloved Puerto Rican poet and revolutionary from Caguas

Betances: Ramón Emiterio Betances, multifaceted revolutionary, doctor, and poet, considered the father of the Puerto Rican independence movement

Borinquén: the Arawak name for the island now known as Puerto Rico

Brillantina: pomade for the hair that was extensively used by men

Caguas: a city and municipality located in the Cordillera Mountains in east-central Puerto Rico, the name is derived from a Taino casique named Caguax

Cagüeño: a native resident of Caguas

Chavos: pennies or money in general

Chango: a commonly found grackle, (Q.n. bracypterus)

Changó: a popular Orisha associated with thunder and sometimes appearing as Santa Bárbara

Cuatro: the Puerto Rican national instrument, originally it had four strings, hence its name, but currently it has ten strings

Colonia: men's cologne

Coquí: is the common onomatopoeic name for a group of small endemic Puerto Rican frogs that fill the night with their music, (Eleutherodactylus)

Cordillera: main mountain range in Puerto Rico that runs east to west and divides the island into northern and southern coastal plains

Doña Lola: Lola Rodríguez de Tió, Puerto Rican activist and poet

Eleggúa: an Orisha associated with Saint Anthony or Saint Michael

Guagua: Puerto Rican word for bus

Guayabera: typically a man's shirt that is used formally, or informally, throughout the Caribbean and equatorial Spanish-speaking regions

Guineos: Puerto Rican word for bananas

Güiro: percussion instrument made out of a hollow gourd

Habichelas: Puerto Rican word for beans

LLoréns Torres: Puerto Rican poet, playwright, and a leader of the independent movement of the island

Loíza: Small town and municipality in the northeastern part of the island, there is not real agreement as to where the name comes from, some say it was from a female cacique named Yuíza

Luquillo: public beach and municipality in the northeastern part of the island, name is derived from a casique named Loquillo

Mancha de plátano: the plantain stain, an expression that came from a poem by Luis LLoréns Torres and which means that you can't erase your "Puerto Ricaness"

Mangó: accent denotes Puerto Rican pronunciation of the name

Mantecado: Puerto Rican word meaning ice-cream

Mofongo: a dish made with fried green plantains, then smashed with garlic, olive oil, and pork crackling

Ñame: a kind of yam

Pastelillos: similar to an empanada, but fried and filled with diverse ingredients

Pisicorre: is a small van utilized as a bus with is capacity for 12-14 passengers but in actuality, drivers add wooden benches to increase the number of passengers; often these buses are filled to double capacity, and are best known for the excessive speed and erratic crisscrossing in heavy traffic.

Pitorro: a distilled spirit from Puerto Rico, "moonshine rum," with a high alcohol content

Plaza Palmer: plaza of the city of Caguas on the original center, it began being built around 1814

Santa Bárbara: catholic saint syncretized with Changó, a powerful male Orisha

Santerísmo: a religion merging African and catholic believes

Taíno: the original inhabitants of the island of Borinquén now known as Puerto Rico

Ta'ca'detra': está acá detrás, Puerto Ricans are known to cut the first syllables of words and attach them to the following word, which is also missing the first syllable, making it a bit difficult for non-Puerto Ricans to understand the colloquialism

Tapones: traffic jams

Tembleque: a Puerto Rican dessert similar to a coconut pudding

Tostones: fried green plantains

Vejigante: a folkloric character most often seen during carnival but dating back to Cervantes times

Yoruba: a West African ethnic group that was sold into slavery in the Caribbean

Yocahú: in the dualistic belief of the Tainos, this was their god of good

Yunque: a high peak in the northeast section of the Cordillera Mountains in Puerto Rico, (3543 feet), known for its rainforest environment and preservation

ABOUT THE AUTHOR

Born in Mexico and raised in Puerto Rico, Amelia Díaz Ettinger has written poems that reflect the struggle with identity often found in immigrants. She began writing poetry at age three by dictating her poems out loud to her uncles who wrote them down for her. Amelia continued writing poems and short stories throughout her life. Her writing took a back seat while she raised two wonderful human beings and worked as a high school teacher. Now retired, she has renewed her writing with fervor. She currently resides in Summerville, Oregon with her husband Chip, her dog Pi, and seven unnamed chickens.

www.ameliaettinger.wordpress.com

ACKNOWLEDGMENTS

Many people helped in bringing this book to life. My deepest gratitude goes to George Venn for his wise advice and careful editing of these poems. Also to Dave Memmott and Peter Sears for believing in me as a writer and getting me back to writing after a twenty-four year hiatus. Thanks also to Kristin Summers of redbat books for her patience and dedication to the completion of this endeavour.

I also would like to thank my husband Chip and our son Luke, both who sat through endless readings and whose critiques added insight and honesty to the work. To my daughter Mariel, *gracias hija por tu fe en la identidad latina.*

Thanks also to Robert Stubblefield editor of *Oregon East Literary Journal*, Vol. XXIII, where the following poems first appeared:
    "Sunday at the Races"
    "Ode to the Mango"

Finally, thanks to my two adoptive cities, Caguas, Puerto Rico and La Grande, Oregon, whose essence serve as a constant source of inspiration.

For other titles available from redbat books, please visit:
www.redbatbooks.com

Also available through Ingram's, Amazon.com,
Barnesandnoble.com, Powells.com and by special order
through your local bookstore.

CPSIA information can be obtained at www.ICGtesting.com
Printed in the USA
LVOW10s1931151015

458475LV00004B/181/P